D1121578

Kelley, J. A., 1954–
Meteor showers /

c2010.
33305218342487
mi   01/07/10

Meteor Showers

J. A. KELLEY

Children's Press®
A Division of Scholastic Inc.
New York Toronto London Auckland Sydney
Mexico City New Delhi Hong Kong
Danbury, Connecticut

Content Consultant
Noreen Grice
Astronomer
President, You Can Do Astronomy, LLC.
www.youcandoastronomy.com

Library of Congress Cataloging-in-Publication Data

Kelley, J. A., 1954-
  Meteor Showers / by J.A. Kelley.
      p. cm. — (A true book)
  Includes index.
  ISBN 13: 978-0-531-16897-4 (lib. bdg.)   978-0-531-22804-3 (pbk.)
  ISBN 10: 0-531-16897-2 (lib. bdg.)   0-531-22804-5 (pbk.)

1. Meteor showers — Juvenile literature. I. Title. II. Series.

  QB741.5.K45 2010
  523.5'3 — dc22   2008049668

No part of this publication may be reproduced in whole or in part, or stored in a retrieval system, or transmitted in any form or by any means, electronic, mechanical, photocopying, recording, or otherwise, without written permission of the publisher. For information regarding permission, write to Scholastic Inc., Attention: Permissions Department, 557 Broadway, New York, NY 10012. Produced by Weldon Owen Education Inc.

© 2010 Scholastic Inc.

All rights reserved. Published in 2010 by Children's Press, an imprint of Scholastic Inc. Published simultaneously in Canada. Printed in China.
SCHOLASTIC, CHILDREN'S PRESS, A TRUE BOOK, and associated logos are trademarks and/or registered trademarks of Scholastic Inc.

1 2 3 4 5 6 7 8 9 10 R 19 18 17 16 15 14 13 12 11 10   62

Find the Truth!

Everything you are about to read is true *except* for one of the sentences on this page.

Which one is **TRUE**?

T or F Meteor showers can't be seen from the moon.

T or F Meteorology is the study of meteorites.

Find the answers in this book.

Contents

Meteorite hitting Earth

During the great meteor storm of 1833, more than 150,000 meteors fell in an hour.

THE **BIG** TRUTH!

Looking for Meteor Showers

Meteorite

The Mauna Kea Observatory, in Hawaii, is the world's largest observatory.

CHAPTER 1

Showers of Light

A shooting star isn't really a star at all. The streak of light racing across the sky, and thought by people to be a shooting star, is actually called a **meteor** (MEE-tee-ur). A meteor is created when an object in space heats up from **friction** (FRIK-shuhn) on entry into Earth's **atmosphere** (AT-mu-sfihr).

The Mauna Kea Observatory has some of the largest telescopes in the world.

Meteor Showers

One or two meteors may be visible on a perfectly clear and dark night. But at special times of the year, dozens of meteors can be seen in an hour. This is called a meteor shower. Meteor showers are some of the most amazing sights that can be viewed in the sky above Earth.

On one night in November 1833, thousands of meteors appeared in the sky. People were afraid and some of them thought the world was coming to an end. Scientists have now discovered the reasons for these streaks of light. Meteors have taught them a lot. They have even revealed information about how our own **solar system** (SOH-lur SISS-tuhm) began.

Some meteors are so bright that you can see them during the day.

In this photograph, the meteors look like vertical streaks of light.

Meteroids travelling in space reach speeds of up to 26 miles (42 kilometers) per second.

CHAPTER 2

Space Rocks

Meteoroids (MEE-tee-uh-ROIDS) are objects in space that can be as small as a grain of sand or as large as a boulder. When a meteoroid falls through Earth's atmosphere, friction causes it to heat up. The streak of light we see as it enters Earth's atmosphere, and that some people call a "shooting star," is a meteor.

Meteoroids speed through space more than 2,500 times faster than a baseball fast pitch!

Finding Space Rocks

The Sun, planets, and moons in our solar system formed 4.6 billion years ago. At that time, dust and chunks of rock floated in space. Scientists call these giant rocks **asteroids** (AS-tuh-roids). Sometimes asteroids bump into each other and break up into smaller pieces.

The solar system is only a small part of a vast universe. All the planets in the solar system move in the same direction around the Sun.

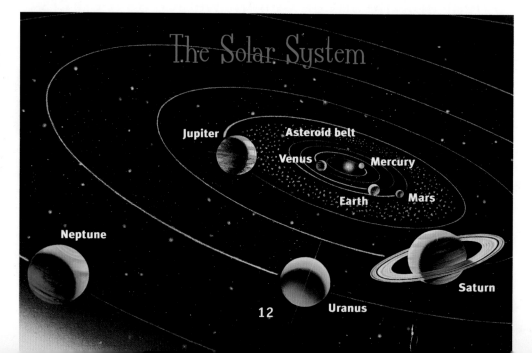

The Solar System

Jupiter

Asteroid belt

Venus

Mercury

Earth

Mars

Neptune

Saturn

Uranus

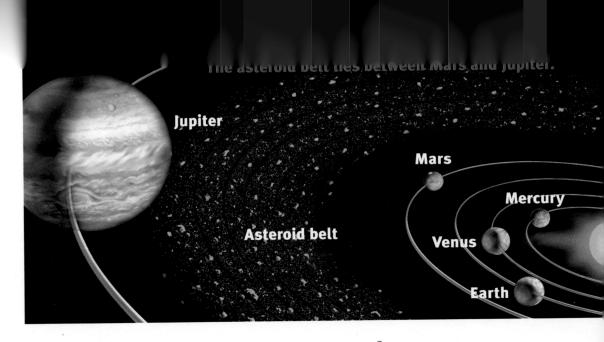

The asteroid belt lies between Mars and Jupiter.

Jupiter

Mars

Mercury

Asteroid belt

Venus

Earth

Most of all known asteroids in our solar system come from the asteroid belt.

Many of the meteoroids that are pulled to Earth are from the asteroid belt between Mars and Jupiter. The **gravitational pull** of Jupiter prevented a planet from forming where the asteroid belt is. It is believed that meteoroids may also exist in the Kuiper (KYE-pur) Belt. This area beyond the planet Neptune is filled with space rocks and chunks of ice.

This picture shows how meteoroids hitting Earth billions of years ago may have looked.

14

CHAPTER 3

The Trip to Earth

Meteoroids don't really fall to Earth. They get pulled in by Earth's gravity. Gravity is an invisible force that pulls one object toward another object. It's what makes Earth and all the other planets orbit, or move, around the Sun.

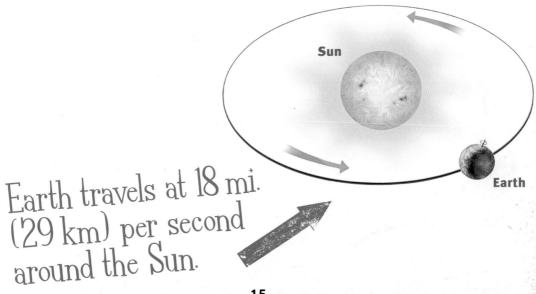

Earth travels at 18 mi. (29 km) per second around the Sun.

Push and Pull

In space, asteroids, **comets**, and meteoroids orbit the Sun, too. If an asteroid bumps into a meteoroid, it pushes the meteoroid into a new orbit. Sometimes its new orbit passes near Earth. Then the meteoroid gets pulled in by our planet's gravity.

Comet Shoemaker Levy-9 was originally orbiting the Sun. After it got caught in Jupiter's gravity, the two collided in 1994.

Burning Up

When a meteoroid nears Earth, it enters our atmosphere. The atmosphere is a mix of gases that surrounds our planet. The meteoroid speeds through these gases and heats up due to friction between the meteoroid and the atmosphere. This raises the temperature of the meteoroid thousands of degrees and causes the surface of it to get worn down. The light from this friction is what is seen when someone on Earth spots a meteor. Meteors could not be seen without an atmosphere. The moon has no atmosphere. Even though it's been hit with millions of space rocks, the streak of light we call a meteor will never be seen on the moon.

Tough Landing

Meteoroids hit the atmosphere at speeds up to 158,400 mi. (249,126 km) per hour. Most meteoroids never actually make it to the ground. Small meteoroids burn up completely. Large meteoroids explode in the atmosphere and break into pieces. These pieces don't always burn up. Once a meteoroid hits Earth's surface, it's called a **meteorite** (MEE-tee-uh-RITE).

About 26,000 meteorites that are larger than a pebble land on Earth each year.

The Willamette Meteorite

The Willamette Meteorite is the largest meteorite found in the United States and the sixth largest meteorite in the world. It was discovered by an Oregon farmer in 1902. It weighs 15.5 tons (14 metric tons). Today the Willamette Meteorite is displayed at the American Museum of Natural History in New York City.

Inside a Meteorite

Not all meteorites are made of the same material. Some come from comets while others come from asteroids. Meteorites can be made mostly of iron (iron meteorites) or stone (stony meteorites). They can also be a combination of both (stony-iron meteorites). Some meteorites even have tiny diamonds that may have come from exploding stars.

This rare iron meteorite was found in Namibia, a country in Africa.

Stony-iron meteorite

Stony meteorite

Other meteorites contain small, round grains called chondrules (KON-druhls). Chondrules are dust **particles** that were heated to very high temperatures when the solar system first formed. Scientists think chondrules were once as hot as 2,000°F (3,600°C). Meteorites containing chondrules are sometimes called the building blocks of the solar system.

Some meteor showers occur every year and they are given names. This is the Perseid meteor shower which happens in August.

CHAPTER 4

Showers in the Forecast

The Earth's gravity is always pulling meteoroids into our atmosphere. On some nights, scientists know that we'll see dozens of meteors in an hour. That's because big meteor showers happen around the same time every year.

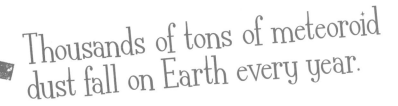

Thousands of tons of meteoroid dust fall on Earth every year.

Comets and Meteor Showers

Each year, Earth travels around its orbit in space. During certain days of the year, Earth crosses the orbit of a comet. Comets are balls of rock, dust, and ice that orbit the Sun. The orbit of a comet is different from that of a planet. One comet may pass by the Sun every few years. Another comet may take a few thousand years to return to the Sun.

As a comet gets closer to the Sun, its ice burns off as gas. The rocks and dust in the ice are left behind in space. These meteoroids form a trail. When Earth moves through the trail left by a comet, the meteoroids enter Earth's atmosphere and we see a meteor shower. If a large comet has recently passed by, more than a thousand meteors per hour can be seen. This unusual event is called a meteor storm.

This comet is called Halley's Comet.
It passes by the Sun every 76 years.

AUGUST

Name: **Perseids**
Best Viewing Dates: **August 11–13**
Comet: **Swift-Tuttle**

APRIL

Name: **Lyrids**
Best Viewing Dates: **April 21–23**
Comet: **Thatcher**

MAY

Name: **Eta Aquarids**
Best Viewing Dates: **May 4–6**
Comet: **Halley**

JULY

AUGUST

OCTOBER

Name: **Draconids**
Best Viewing Dates: **October 7–9**
Comet: **Giacobini-Zinner**

Name: **Orionids**
Best Viewing Dates: **October 20–22**
Comet: **Halley**

NOVEMBER

Name: **Leonids**
Best Viewing Dates: **November 16–18**
Comet: **Tempel-Tuttle**

DECEMBER

Name: **Ursids**
Best Viewing Dates: **December 21–23**
Comet: **Tuttle**

NOVEMBER

Name: **Leonids**
Best Viewing Dates: **November 16–18**
Comet: **Tempel-Tuttle**

Looking for Meteor Showers

Major meteor showers happen around the same time every year. The chart below lists some well-known ones. Meteor showers are named after constellations, or star patterns, from which the meteors appear to be coming.

JANUARY

Name:
Best Vie
Comet:

JANUARY

Name: **Quadrantids**
Best Viewing Dates: **January 2–4**
Comet: **Unnamed**

FEBRUARY

MA

27

The Gibeon meteorites were found in Namibia, Africa. Some of them are on display in this fountain in Namibia's capital city. The meteorites came from a meteor shower more than 200 million years ago.

CHAPTER 5

Pieces of the Past

Early scientists thought that meteors were weather events like snow or rain. Scientist Edmond Halley studied them and figured out that they were related to comets. Records of comets and meteor showers go back for thousands of years.

In 1992, a boy in Uganda was hit on the head by a small meteorite.

On the Record

In 1794, a scientist named Ernst Chladni (KLADNI) wrote about meteorites. Chladni was the first to say that meteorites came from space, but no one believed him. When thousands of meteorites fell on a town in northern France in 1803, scientists noticed they were different from other Earth rocks. Some had black crusts, as if they had been burned. Others were made of dense iron. Scientists accepted the idea that these meteorites were rocks from space.

In 1992, the Peekskill meteorite was seen by thousands of people on the East Coast of the United States. It fell right through the trunk of this car.

Halley's Comet

Edmond Halley studied comets that were seen in 1456, 1531, 1607, and 1682. He noticed that they all had similar orbits. In 1705, Halley published a book that said that all of these were the same comet.

He predicted that this same comet would return in 1758. Halley died in 1742, but the comet reappeared on Christmas 1758. It was named Halley's Comet in his honor.

Edmond Halley was an English mathematician and astronomer. Astronomers study objects in space.

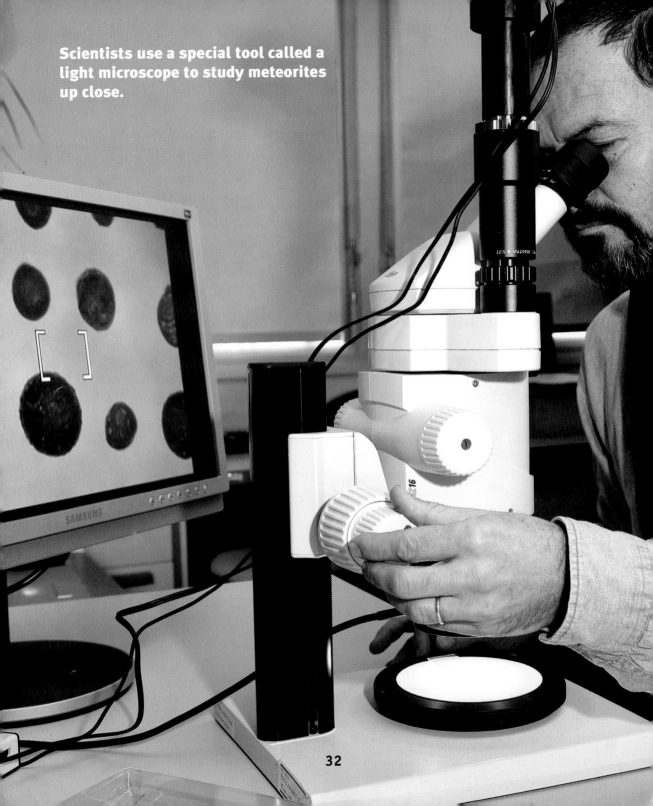

Scientists use a special tool called a light microscope to study meteorites up close.

CHAPTER 6

Learning from Meteorites

Scientists have learned a lot about our universe from studying meteorites. The study of meteorites is called **meteoritics** (mee-tee-uh-RIT-iks). When scientists study meteorites, they look at pieces of rock that haven't changed since the solar system began.

Nomad is a robot designed to search for meteorites in Antarctica.

Signs of Life

Scientists have found some surprising things inside meteorites. Their discoveries have included water as well as other substances found in living creatures on Earth. If such things are found inside rocks from space, then these substances must exist in places other than Earth. This means that life might exist somewhere else in the universe.

Mars Meteorite ALH84001

16 million years ago
An asteroid hits Mars. Pieces of Mars fall into space and become meteoroids.

13,000 years ago
One meteoroid is captured by Earth's gravity and pulled to Earth.

The Meteorite from Mars

Millions of years ago, an object hit the surface of Mars so hard that pieces of it flew up and escaped the planet's gravity. One piece was pulled down by Earth's gravity and was discovered in Antarctica. Scientists named it ALH84001. At first, they thought this meteorite contained traces of tiny bacteria. This would have proved that life existed on Mars. After further study, scientists decided that the bacteria may have entered the meteorite on Earth instead.

1984
Scientist Roberta Score finds a meteorite on Antarctica.

1993
Scientist Donald Mittlefehldt studies the meteorite's gas bubbles. He discovers that it came from Mars!

Meteor Craters

When a large meteorite hits Earth, a **crater** is formed. There are more than 150 meteor craters scattered around the planet. The largest is near the town of Vredefort (FREAR-duh-fort) in South Africa. It measures about 186 mi. (300 km) across. Scientists believe that the meteorite that made the crater was about 6 mi. (10 km) wide.

The Meteor Crater in Arizona was created when a meteorite crashed into Earth about 50,000 years ago. It is about 4,000 ft. (1,200 meters) across.

Scientists have learned a lot by studying the rocks and soil in and around craters. They can tell how long ago a meteorite landed there. They can research how the heat and pressure of a meteorite explosion changes rocks. When they have drilled under craters, scientists have found large deposits of minerals. This has told them that some craters were once filled with water.

Tracing Asteroids

Scientists know that asteroids have hit Earth before. One crashed into our planet 65 million years ago. Some scientists believe this is what caused dinosaurs to become extinct. Today, scientists use telescopes and cameras to track an asteroid as it orbits the Sun. After studying it, they can tell if the asteroid will pass near Earth.

Scientists believe that a giant asteroid hits Earth every 100 million years.

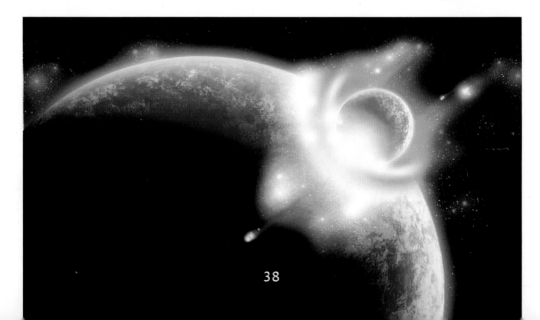

Scientists with the SPACEWATCH™ project at Kitt Peak Observatory in Arizona scan the solar system for Near Earth Objects.

Near Earth Objects

Near Earth Objects (NEOs) are comets and asteroids whose paths cross Earth's orbit and come into Earth's neighborhood. So far, scientists have found more than 5,900 NEOs. More than 750 of these are less than 1 mi. (less than 1 km) or just a little larger across.

These are the four largest asteroids ever discovered. They are placed against a map of the United States to show how big they are.

Ceres Vesta Pallas Hygiea

Studies in Space

Even though Earth is safe for now, scientists want to be prepared. They don't want to wait for an asteroid to come towards us. Instead, scientists study them in space. They've sent spacecraft to get a closer look at asteroids and comets. On February 12, 2001, a robot spacecraft called *NEAR Shoemaker* landed on the Near Earth Object named Eros. It sent information back to scientists on Earth.

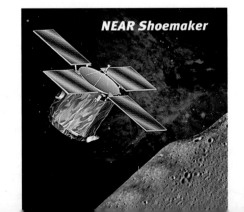

NEAR Shoemaker

40

Solar Sails

How could we keep an asteroid from hitting Earth? A small explosion in space could move an asteroid and send it in a different direction. This could ultimately change an asteroid's path by thousands of miles in a year. One idea is to attach a solar sail to the asteroid. Energy from the Sun would push the asteroid into a safer orbit.

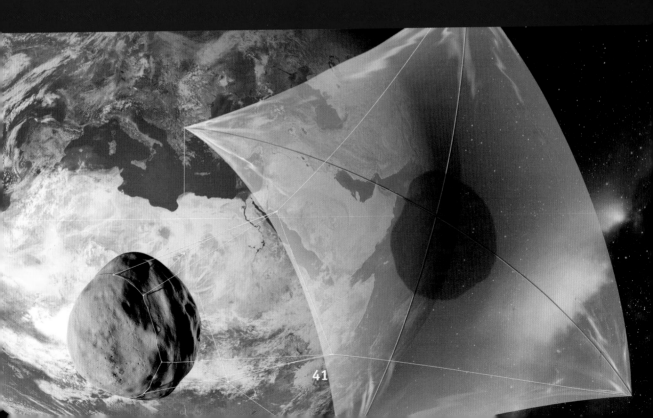

Collecting Dust

The *Stardust* spacecraft was sent to collect dust from the Comet Wild 2 in 1999. Wild 2 passes Earth about every six years. After traveling 3 billion mi. (4.6 billion km) into space, *Stardust* returned to Earth in 2006. Scientists continue to study these samples and many other meteorites to learn more about the universe. ★

Stardust

Samples collected by *Stardust* from Comet Wild 2 have helped scientists learn about how the solar system began.

True Statistics

Number of meteorites found on Earth: 22,000

Known meteorites from Mars: 34

Point where meteors start to glow: 40 mi. (65 km) above Earth's surface

Most meteors ever observed in a meteor shower: More than 150,000 per hour

Amount of space rocks and dust that falls on Earth each year: Between 44–175 million lb. (20–80 million kg)

Weight of largest known iron meteorite: 119,050 lb. (54,000 kg)

Did you find the truth?

(T) Meteor showers can't be seen from the moon.

(F) Meteorology is the study of meteorites.

Resources

Books

Bortz, Fred. *Collision Course!: Cosmic Impacts and Life on Earth.* Brookfield, CT: Millbrook Press, 2001.

Chrismer, Melanie. *Comets.* New York: Children's Press, 2005.

Kerrod, Robin. *Asteroids, Comets, and Meteors (Planet Library).* Minneapolis, MN: Lerner Publications Company, 2000.

Koppes, Steven N. *Killer Rocks From Outer Space: Asteroids, Comets, and Meteorites.* Minneapolis, MN: Lerner Publications Company, 2004.

Landau, Elaine. *Beyond Pluto.* New York: Children's Press, 2008.

Man, John. *Comets, Meteors, and Asteroids.* New York: DK Publishing, 2001.

Spangenburg, Ray, and Kit Moser. *Meteors, Meteorites, and Meteoroids (Out of This World).* New York: Franklin Watts, 2002.

Stott, Carole. *The World of Astronomy.* New York: Kingfisher Publications, 2006.

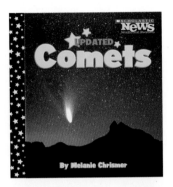

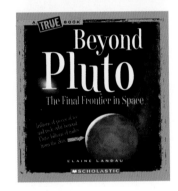

Organizations and Web Sites

StarDate Online: Meteor Showers
www.stardate.org/nightsky/meteors
Learn the best viewing dates and times for meteor showers.

NASA/JPL Mars Meteorites
www.jpl.nasa.gov/snc
Read all about the meteorites from Mars.

Windows to the Universe
www.windows.ucar.edu
Check out this site for more information about meteors, and play games and puzzles.

Places to Visit

Peabody Museum of Natural History
Yale University
170 Whitney Avenue
New Haven, CT 06511
(203) 432 5050
www.peabody.yale.edu
Visit one of the oldest meteorite collections in the United States.

Meteor Crater
Interstate 40, at exit 233
Winslow, AZ 86047
(928) 289 2362
www.meteorcrater.com
Visit a crater that was formed by a meteorite about 50,000 years ago.

Important Words

asteroids (AS-tuh-roids) – large pieces of rock and metal that orbit the Sun

atmosphere (AT-mu-sfihr) – the blanket of gases that surrounds a planet or other object

comets – balls of rock, dust, and ice that orbit the Sun

crater – a hole in the surface of a planet or moon formed by the force of a meteorite

friction (FRIK-shuhn) – the force that slows down an object whenever it touches something else

gravitational pull – the attraction that one object has for another object due to the invisible force of gravity

meteor (MEE-tee-ur) – an object from space that becomes glowing hot when it passes into Earth's atmosphere

meteorite (MEE-tee-uh-RITE) – a piece of rock or metal that reaches Earth's surface

meteoritics (mee-tee-uh-RIT-iks) – the study of meteorites

meteoroids (MEE-tee-uh-ROIDS) – tiny pieces of stone or metal that move through outer space

particles – very small pieces of something

solar system (SOH-lur SISS-tuhm) – a star and all of the objects that travel around it

Index

Page numbers in **bold** indicate illustrations

About the Author

J. A. Kelley is a writer of nonfiction books and articles for children. Although she writes on many different subjects, Ms. Kelley is especially interested in meteors. In fact, a famous meteor shower occurs on her birthday every year. Ms. Kelley is a graduate of Northwestern University and lives in Brooklyn, New York, with her husband and daughter.

PHOTOGRAPHS © 2008: AAPimage.com /AP/Beth A. Keiser (p. 19); Big Stock Photo (©Dusan Zidar, p. 3; ©Jim Mills, stony meteorite, p. 21); Dreamstime (©Dmitry Kutlayev, binoculars, p. 27; ©Sean Gladwell, asteroid hitting Mars, p. 34); Dutch Meteor Society (p. 29); iStockphoto (©Andrew Whittle, pp. 36–37; ©Dominika Gardocka, p. 10; ©James Thew, p. 38; ©Stephan Hoerold, back cover, p. 18; ©Strathroy, stony iron meteorite, p. 21); NASA (p. 33; meteorite, p. 35: NEAR Shoemaker, p. 40; Ames Research Center/S. Molau & P. Jenniskens, perseids, p. 26; Caltech/J. Vaubaillon, quadrantids, p. 27; J.C. Casado & I. Graboleda, leonids, p. 26; JPL: Jet Propulsion Laboratory, p. 42; Pierre Thomas (LST)/ENS Lyon, p. 30; ©Wally Pacholka, p. 34); Photolibrary (cover; meteorite, p. 5; p. 6; p. 9; p. 14; p. 20; p. 25; pp. 31–32; p. 39; largest asteroids, p. 40; p. 41); photonewzealand/alamy (p. 28); Tranz (Corbis, meteor storm, p. 5; Reuters, p. 22)